TERRY FOX

RUNNING TO THE HEART OF CANADA

SHELDON POSEN   ERIN GURSKI

"... right now I can look back
and think of all the good
things that happened and the
good people I met

CANADIAN MUSEUM OF HISTORY
MUSÉE CANADIEN DE L'HISTOIRE

Library and Archives Canada
Cataloguing in Publication

Posen, Sheldon
Terry Fox: running to the heart of Canada /
Sheldon Posen, Erin Gurski.

(Souvenir catalogue series, 2291-6385)
Issued also in French under title:
Terry Fox, courir au cœur du Canada.
ISBN 978-0-660-20310-2
Cat. no.: NM23-5/12-2015E

1. Fox, Terry, 1958-1981.
2. Canadian Museum of History – Exhibitions.
3. Runners (Sports) – Canada – Biography.
4. Cancer – Patients – Canada – Biography.
I.   Gurski, Erin.
II. Canadian Museum of History.
III. Title.
IV. Title: Running to the heart of Canada.
V.   Series: Souvenir catalogue series.

RC265.6 F68 P67 2015
362.196'994410092
C2015-980000-5

Published by the
Canadian Museum of History
100 Laurier Street
Gatineau, QC K1A 0M8
historymuseum.ca

Printed and bound in Canada.

This work is a souvenir of the exhibition
Terry Fox - Running to the Heart of Canada,
 which was organized by the Canadian Museum
of History, in partnership with the Terry Fox Centre.

Cover image:
© Gail Harvey

Souvenir Catalogue series, 12
ISSN 2291-6385

CONTENTS

FOREWORD

In the pages that follow, you will revisit the stirring and bittersweet moment in Canadian history when a young man with a big dream, an iron will and a noble cause captured the heart of a nation and secured an enduring place in our national consciousness.

This souvenir catalogue — and the exhibition on which it is based — tells the story of Terry's life on the road during his Marathon of Hope, and explores the unique and abiding bond he forged with the Canadian people.

Little notice was taken on April 12, 1980, when the earnest 21-year-old dipped his artificial leg into the Atlantic Ocean and began his run toward the Pacific. His twin goals of running a marathon a day and collecting $1 from every Canadian for cancer research and awareness seemed ambitious at best. But less than 5 months later, Terry Fox was a household name.

He had raised over $23 million and was adored and admired throughout the country for his tenacity and humility, his commitment to a larger cause and his daily triumph over adversity. Terry Fox had struck a chord in Canada's soul. It reverberates still.

As Canadians mark the 35th anniversary of the Marathon of Hope, the Canadian Museum of History, working in partnership with the Terry Fox Centre, is pleased to present a unique and intimate account of Terry's odyssey and legacy. The three identities that bear the Terry Fox name, together with the Fox family, strive to keep his memory alive, to inspire others to carry on his legacy, and to help fulfill his dream of finding a cure for cancer. In the same spirit, the Museum strives to enhance public understanding of events, experiences and people that reflect and have shaped our country's history and identity. Terry Fox and the Marathon of Hope deserve a prominent place on any such list.

Mark O'Neill

President and
Chief Executive Officer
Canadian Museum of History

"I never gave up, right from the beginning."

INTRODUCTION

His story is now part of Canada's own.

In March 1977, Terry Fox, 18, of Port Coquitlam, British Columbia, lost his right leg to cancer. While undergoing chemotherapy in a children's ward, Terry watched other young patients suffer and die. He survived and, haunted by this experience, he resolved to do something to combat the disease: "Somewhere," he later wrote, "the hurting must stop."

Always an athlete, Terry devised a plan to run across Canada and raise money for cancer research. He trained himself to run on his artificial leg, and spent more than a year building strength and stamina.

"I trained as hard as I think you can train for it. Christmas Day was my first day off in 101 days. In that time I ran with the flu, shin splints, bone bruises, you name it I had it. And I ran through that at that time because I felt I had to build my confidence before my trip . . . Because I knew when I ran across Canada I was going to encounter the same things."

Terry approached the Canadian Cancer Society and won its backing. The Society's Ron Calhoun dubbed the project the Marathon of Hope. The Ford Motor Company of Canada provided a van. And Terry convinced his best friend, Doug Alward, to join him as driver and road companion.

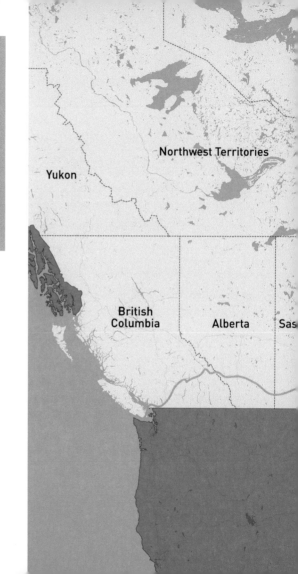

Proposed Route
for the Marathon of Hope

Nunavut

wan   Manitoba

Ontario   Quebec   Newfoundland

New Brunswick
                                 Prince Edward Island

United States   Nova Scotia

13

"One thing about Doug, I knew I could depend on him. And I could depend on him to do anything to help me."

On April 12, 1980, Terry and Doug set out from St. John's, Newfoundland. Terry planned to run along the Trans-Canada Highway to Vancouver, British Columbia, raising money for the Canadian Cancer Society as he went. The Society's goal was $100,000.

The amount raised was $23.4 million.

The overwhelming success of the Marathon of Hope was due to the extraordinary response of Canadians to an extraordinary young man.

Over the 143 days of the run, Canadians came to idealize Terry Fox as the embodiment of the virtues they prized most — courage, integrity, tenacity, selflessness. And at a time when Quebec was deciding whether to remain in Canada, and Canada was one of the countries boycotting the 1980 Summer Olympics, Terry was regarded as a force for national unity and his run as "the real Olympics."

Canadians took to him personally. Terry had a charming, self-deprecating magnetism and a youthful, noble bearing which captured people's hearts. In the thousands of cards and letters they sent him, many wrote as if Terry were their son or brother or best friend; some said they felt he was running for them. In conversations across Canada, he was simply, affectionately, "Terry."

On September 1, 1980, just over halfway home, Terry's cancer returned and he was forced to stop running.

But in what now seems a very Canadian gesture, people made Terry's effort rather than his "success" what counted. Success was, in fact, ensured by them.

As if it were the most natural thing in the world, Canadians took up Terry's cause as a passing of the torch. Thousands of people ran marathons and held fundraisers. By the time Terry died on June 28, 1981, the Marathon of Hope coffers were filled to overflowing.

Soon afterwards, annual September "runs for Terry" were initiated as local events across Canada. Over the years, these runs — now organized nationally and internationally by the Terry Fox Foundation — have raised some $650 million in Terry's name for cancer research.

The story of Terry Fox is part of everyday life in Canada, part of the collective memory, part of how Canadians teach their children what a hero is.

Scrapbooks

Even during the run itself, Canadians were making Terry Fox's story their own. They put together Marathon of Hope scrapbooks, pasting in newspaper clippings about his daily runs as a way of capturing its spirit and excitement. Through such collections, his followers could hold Terry and his journey in their hands. In the end, sadly, their scrapbooks became personal memorials to his heartbreaking triumph.

When Terry passed away, many Canadians sent their scrapbooks to his parents, Betty and Rolly Fox. It was as if to say (and some did), "Here is something of your son, whom we watched every day with awe, gratitude and pride. We send these now with our admiration and love."

MARATHON

OF

HOPE

Marathon of Hope

Terry Fox is a 21 year old resident of
Port Coquitlam, B.C. and he believes
in miracles - he has to! Two and a
half years ago Terry lost his right leg
to Cancer. Today, after a courageous
fight back, he is jogging across
Canada in a determined effort to
raise funds through sponsorship to
generate money for advancing Cancer Research. He is reaching out to
you and me to join him in his bold en-
deavour by a companion jog in your
area and or your financial support in
this his—MARATHON OF HOPE

Index - July 28 - 00 upm
approached our area.

Scrap Book

MARATHON

OF

HOPE

TERRY   FOX

Canada the Beautiful...
Running with Terry Fox

To Terry
with love

It is in this same spirit that we offer this book.

It contains images from those scrapbooks, along with the work of some of the photographers who immortalized the Marathon of Hope.

Most of the words are those of Terry Fox, taken from his daily journal, or transcribed from speeches he made over the course of the run or from interviews he gave to journalists such as Leslie Scrivener.

This is a Terry Fox memory book. It takes the reader back to 143 days in 1980 when Canadians watched, marvelled and idolized, then mourned and celebrated a heroic young athlete running in a noble cause to the heart of Canada.

Sheldon Posen   Erin Gurski

Gatineau, Quebec
April 1, 2015

NEWFOUNDLAND

April 12 to May 6
25 Days
576 Miles

Marathon Total:
576 Miles

Corner Brook 19

25 Port aux Basques

Marathon of Hope
Newfoundland
Actual Route

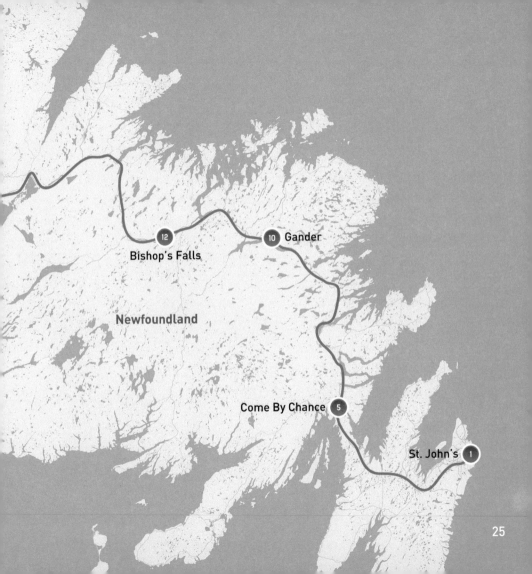

Newfoundland

Bishop's Falls 12

Gander 10

Come By Chance 5

St. John's 1

"Today is the day
it all begins."

"I went to Logy Bay to get
some Atlantic Ocean H_2O.

We got to Trober St.
where we were to start
at around 2:30 p.m. There
were many reporters here
to greet us on our way.
I touched the ocean
before I left."

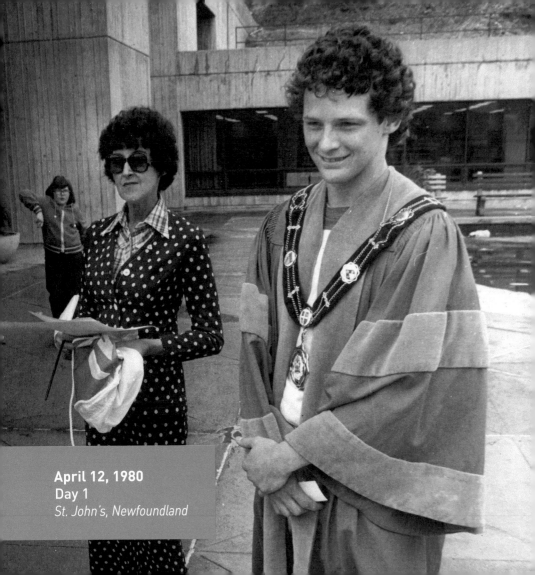

April 12, 1980
Day 1
St. John's, Newfoundland

"I started in St. John's because my home is in B.C. and I wanted to finish at home."

He runs a campaign of courage

Toronto Star
Thursday, April 17, 1980
Section D, pages D1-D24

By Leslie Scrivener
Toronto Star

Nothing, not gale force winds, not pouring rain nor spring snowstorm, not even the lack of a leg is going to stop Terry Fox from running across Canada.

"I come from a competitive, stubborn family," says the 21-year-old university student from Port Coquitlam, B.C., who lost his right leg to cancer three years ago. "I have to prove to myself that even though my leg was amputated, I am not disabled. I am not going to let myself down."

His journey, to raise pledges for the Canadian Cancer Society, has only just begun. Terry spoke to The Star yesterday from the home of the mayor of Come-By-Chance, Nfld., 93 miles north-west of St. John's where he started his run last Saturday afternoon.

A Simon Fraser University student and former basketball and soccer player, Terry hopes to dip his artificial leg into the Pacific Ocean next fall just as he dipped it in the Atlantic last week. If he keeps a pace of 20 to 30 miles a day he should be on the cedar-lined shores of Stanley Park next October.

Terry says he feels "pretty good" even though his first four days of running on the Trans-Canada Highway were slow, marked by heavy rain, a snowstorm, 40-mile-an-hour winds — "they held me to a standstill, I couldn't move" — and very steep hills.

Glimpses of sea

"But I've heard the hilly country is pretty well over," Terry says in a voice bubbling with confidence. He says the route has been at times barren, at other times heavily treed; occasionally he has had glimpses of the sea. "Tell my Mom we're having some Vancouver weather here," he says.

He also has had to sleep in a bone-cold camper, supplied by the Ford Motor Co., because the propane tanks can't be filled until Clarenville, a town 26 miles away.

The setback he expected, a break-down in his artificial leg, hasn't happened. He's carrying two spares with him and hopes they will see him through the 3½-week crossing of Newfoundland. The War Amputations of Canada organization is supplying and servicing the legs in centres where they have offices.

His only physical complaint so far is a tightening in the thigh muscles.

But Terry is being cheered by motorists, who honk, wave and wish him well, and is warmly welcomed in the tiny Newfoundland whistle stops along the route.

Running with Terry

☐ Terry Fox is a living lesson in courage and determination. Last Saturday, the 21-year-old cancer victim with one leg set out to run 5,000 miles from the Atlantic to the Pacific oceans to prove that cancer can be beaten. The Toronto Star will be running with Terry all the way. Terry will be checking in weekly with The Star. You'll read his progress every Friday in the Family Section, starting next week.

Betty Gilbert, wife of Come-By-Chance's mayor George, stood on the road yesterday and waved Terry down, offering him a hot shower, home-cooked meal and a good bed for the night. She said the town's young people were baking him a cake, buying a gift and planning a surprise party for the brave young runner.

Terry is accompanied by his childhood friend, Doug Alward, also 21 and a student at Simon Fraser University, who drives the van, prepares meals and has fresh clothing laid out. Terry says he wears four shirts, sweat pants, a rain top, toque and gloves in the cold weather. "That's really draining, but I should be really trucking on pretty soon."

Terry's determination dates to 1977 when he was an 18-year-old student in first year kinesiology who learned the pain in his leg was bone cancer. Within a week, his muscular leg was gone from six inches above the knee.

Diagnosed as cancer

The suffering and cancer deaths he saw during follow-up treatment made him all the more determined to help fight the deadly disease that claims one out of every six Canadian lives. In the time it will take to complete his run, it's estimated nearly 40,000 Canadians will be diagnosed as cancer cases.

"I've seen a lot of disability, people who were really shut in and away from life and who couldn't do anything. I want to show that just because they're disabled, it's not the end, in fact, it's more of a challenge," he says.

"In my year and a half of chemotherapy, I lost my hair temporarily, and was very sick, yet I was healthier than anyone I met."

His father, Rolly, a Canadian National Railways switchman and the father of three other children aged 15 to 22, says his son was inspired during his convalescence by a magazine story brought to him by a basketball coach about a one-legged man who ran the New York marathon.

"I decided if he did it, I'm going to do it too," says Terry.

He started training 14 months ago, walking a quarter-mile a day, enduring great pain and blisters, sores and the loss of toenails on his good leg because of the pressure on it.

But he ignored the discomfort, his father says proudly, because at the back of his mind was the single thought of the strong-willed New York runner.

In 1974, Mark Kent, a 17-year-old North York high school student was the first person to run across Canada from coast to coast. Terry will be the first person to run across the country with only one leg.

Last year, Terry ran for 101 consecutive days, training for this cross-country endurance test, and stopped only for Christmas Day, his father says.

"It convinced him he was in very good shape mentally and physically to complete the run," Rolly Fox told The Star from his Port Coquitlam home.

His mother Betty, who manages a card shop, says she worked with her son, laying the groundwork for the journey. He wrote to businesses asking for sponsorship and received support from such companies as Esso, which supplied gas money, Adidas for running equipment, Safeway and the Four Season hotels, among others.

His parents say they believe he can cross Canada if his health endures. His mother, showing a lively maternal concern, says, "I just hope he doesn't push himself too hard. But because of the type of person he is, I think he'll make it.

She says Terry was deeply affected by his experiences in chemotherapy. "He wants to help cancer research. He's seen a lot of young people not make it and that impression stayed with him — of all the suffering he's seen in others."

She proudly adds that throughout the rehabilitation, Terry kept up his school work, receiving all As and Bs and somehow managed to get on the golf course within a month of his operation.

Says his father, simply, reflecting the confidence that seems to be a family trait: "He was brought up to finish what he starts."

From sea to sea: Terry Fox has come 93 miles; he still has about 4,900 to go in his journey from Atlantic to Pacific Ocean. But the 21-year-old who lost his leg to cancer three years ago is determined to prove he is not disabled.

VANCOUVER PROVINCE

**April 16, 1980
Day 5**
*Come By Chance,
Newfoundland*

29

"I phoned the Toronto Star and found that Leslie Scrivener and the Star were behind me. I feel quite lightheaded right now."

"When I got back to my hotel, Leslie Scrivener phoned and told me the Four Seasons Hotel had sponsored me for $2 a mile. And they were going to challenge 1,000 other companies to do the same. Incredible news, an incredible lift."

Let's make Terry's run really count.

Here's how you can help make it a ten million dollar run... for only $2.00 per mile.

1,000 companies each pledging $2.00 per mile for Terry's cross Canada run will raise ten million dollars to help defeat cancer. We're starting this campaign with our pledge of $2.00 per mile. Terry hopes to run a total of about 5,000 miles.

Terry Fox is a 21 year old university student from Port Coquitlam, B.C., who lost his right leg to cancer three years ago. Having started in St. John's, Newfoundland, he plans to run across

Canada this summer to Vancouver to prove that cancer can be beaten. Let's help prove he's right.

You can make your pledge at any branch of the Canadian Cancer Society or by phoning Four Seasons Hotels toll free from anywhere in Canada,
800-268-6282.

We also have pledge boxes in the lobbies of our hotels across Canada for individuals who may also wish to contribute. Every penny counts.

A pledge of one cent a mile would contribute $50.00.

Please help us make Terry's run really count in the battle against cancer.

Four Seasons Hotels

Montreal • Toronto • Ottawa • Belleville • Calgary • Edmonton • Vancouver • Israel • United States
Inn on the Park Toronto • London, England

April 21, 1980
Day 10
Gander, Newfoundland

31

April 23, 1980
Day 12
*Bishop's Falls,
Newfoundland*

"We ran down to where all kinds of school kids and people were waiting. It was a fantastic greeting and reception, and they all gave me an ovation."

"We went to the city hall where I met the mayor and talked with loads of people.

We were given gifts and during the day we collected over $2,000.00 and also all kinds more came in.

It was a fantastic day and a very rewarding one."

April 23, 1980
Day 12
Grand Falls, Newfoundland

"It was 4 miles of uphill into Corner Brook. A very difficult and tiring time, but I made it.

We raised over $7,000.00 here for sure."

TERRY FO[?]
MARATHON
OF
HOPE

T[?] [?]ANADA RUN
CA[?] [?]ESEARCH

[?]RD [?]UNCRAFT ARE
[?]OUD TO BE ASSOCI-
[?]D WITH THIS BRAVE
[?]NDEAVOUR

May 6, 1980
Day 25
Port aux Basques, Newfoundland

"We raised $10,000.00 in Port aux Basques, which is fabulous."

"People in Newfoundland have been great all along. The friendliness of these people is something I'll never forget."

TERRY FO
MARATH
OF
HO

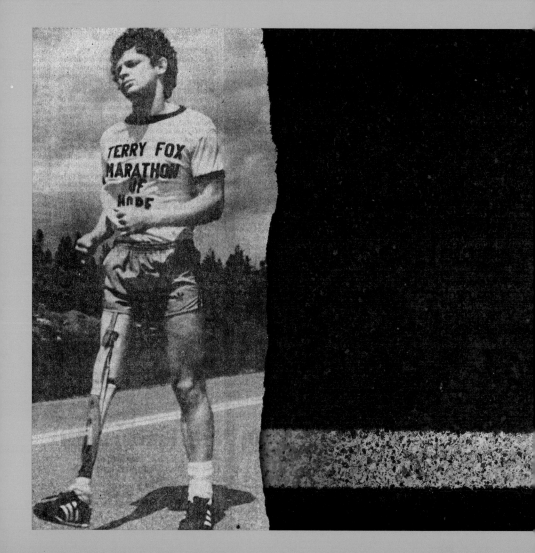

NOVA SCOTIA

May 7 to 22
16 Days
396 Miles

Marathon Total:
972 Miles

Marathon of Hope
Nova Scotia
Actual Route

42

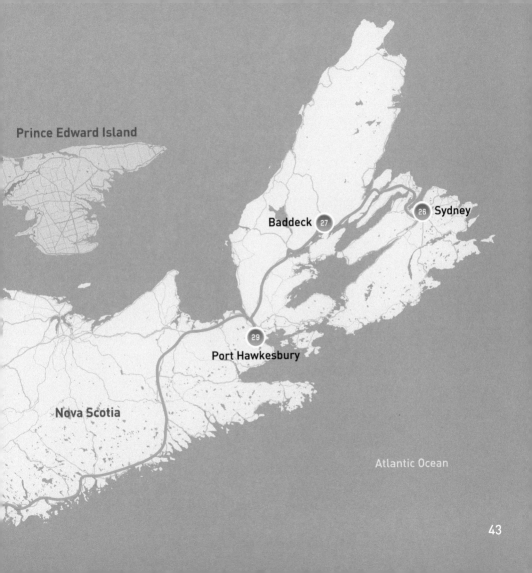

Prince Edward Island

Baddeck 27

26 Sydney

29
Port Hawkesbury

Nova Scotia

Atlantic Ocean

"George Thorn did a marvelous job organizing the day. I ran with a group of school kids to city hall and met the mayor."

May 7, 1980
Day 26
Sydney, Nova Scotia

44

"We finished around 5 miles short of Baddeck. The people were still great. Honking and waving. A great lift."

"Doug has been a pain, we argued all morning."

"We met a Mr. and Mrs. Fox and we had a lovely time."

"They left me a poem on a big piece of paper that I put on the wall that I call, 'I grinned and I did it.' They were great people."

Mayor Billy Joe MacLean and Fire Chief George Fox

May 10, 1980
Day 29
Port Hawkesbury, Nova Scotia

"It Couldn't Be Done"

Somebody said that it couldn't be done,
But, he with a chuckle replied
That "maybe it couldn't," but he would be one
Who wouldn't say so till he'd tried.
So he buckled right in with the trace of a grin
On his face. If he worried he hid it.
He started to sing as he tackled the thing
That couldn't be done, and he did it.

There are thousands to tell you it cannot be done,
There are thousands to prophesy failure;
There are thousands to point out to you one by one,
The dangers that wait to assail you.
But just buckle it in with a bit of a grin,
Just take off your coat and go to it;
Just start to sing as you tackle the thing
That "couldn't be done," and you'll do it.

— **Edgar Albert Guest**

May 20, 1980
Day 39
Halifax, Nova Scotia

48

"I met the mayor in Halifax. The radio station here was of great help."

"I'm pissed off that we're not raising more money. Nothing is being done to raise money anywhere."

"I did my speech and I couldn't help but cry when I said how Doug had to have the courage to put up with and understand me when I'm tired and irritable."

Terry's parents flew in to visit their son and to help Doug and Terry work through their disagreements.

"We drove back to Springhill where we met Ron Jefferson who had done a fantastic job organizing things here. We raised over $1,000.00 here. I was in a bitchy mood unfortunately. I wish I could relax more. Anyways I ran another mile into the City Hall, with fire engines and a police escort. There were a lot of people there to meet me. I did my speech and it went well . . . Ken gave us some good advice. Be disappointed at the fundraising part of it but not mad! I've got to try harder to control myself."

May 22, 1980
Day 41
Springhill, Nova Scotia

"The people have been great, just great, all the way across. Some of the receptions I have had have been tremendous."

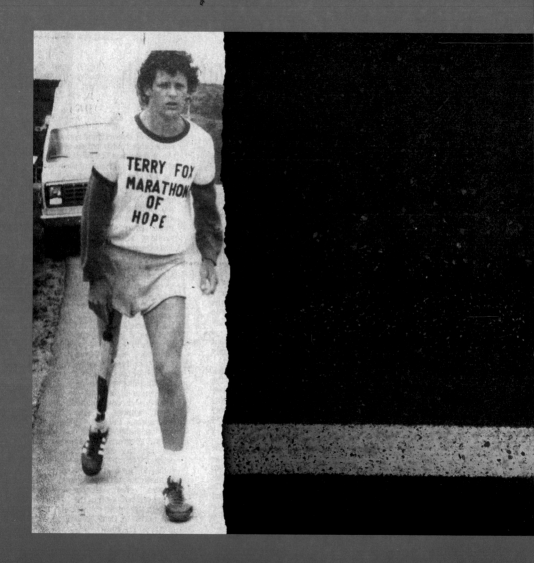

PRINCE EDWARD ISLAND

May 24 to 26
3 Days
74 Miles

Marathon Total:
1,074 Miles

Marathon of Hope
Prince Edward Island
Actual Route

New Brunswick

Nova Scotia

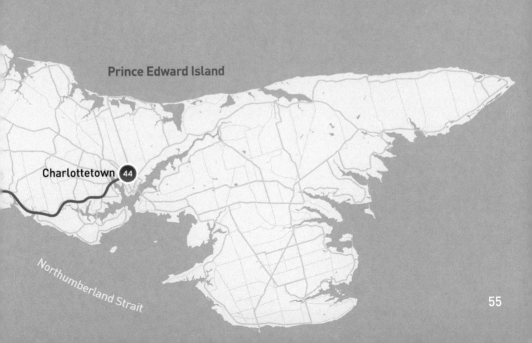

Prince Edward Island

Charlottetown 44

Northumberland Strait

"There were tons of people out to cheer me on and support me. Incredible. We collected over $600.00 on the road today, our best!"

"It was an outstanding reception by a great town and province. It was all set up by two very fine men: Jim Ayre and Jim Cox."

"Still freezing but I wasn't wearing sweats so people could see my leg."

"Prince Edward Island I really enjoyed. We were only there for a day and a quarter and it was just such a fantastic thing. It was so neat to be on such a tiny island and to be able to say I ran through another province so quickly."

NEW BRUNSWICK

May 27 to June 9
14 Days
406 Miles

Marathon Total:
1,452 Miles

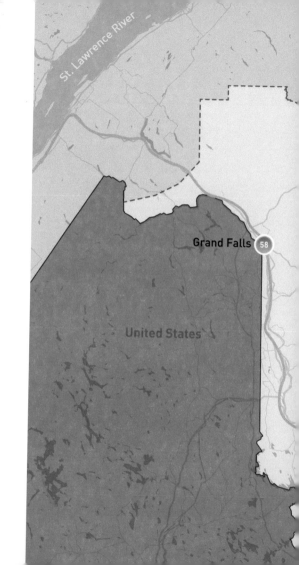

Marathon of Hope
New Brunswick
Actual Route

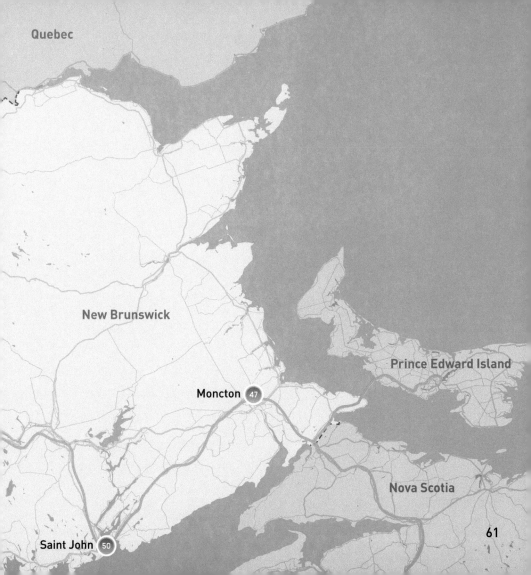

Quebec

New Brunswick

Prince Edward Island

Moncton 47

Nova Scotia

61

Saint John 50

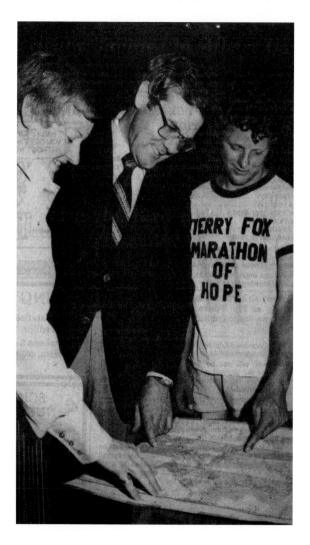

"We ran right through the city of Moncton, down Main Street. We collected a lot of money through here. When one car would start to honk they all would. It was great."

May 28, 1980
Day 47
Moncton, New Brunswick

"Bill Vigars was here
when we awoke.
He has staged interviews.
Very nice fellow."

"It was very
heartwarming
to see Darrell. Brought
a few tears as we
embraced. Got me
moving a bit faster."

In New Brunswick, Terry's
younger brother Darrell joined
the run. The Canadian Cancer
Society's Bill Vigars made a
preliminary visit in preparation
for the Ontario campaign.

"The Jaycees did a wonderful job here. The whole town was there to greet me. I did my speech. They followed me out of town till I did my final 8 miles. It was tremendous support. We did very well fundraising as well."

"New Brunswick is about the most beautiful I've seen so far . . . and the people here are unbelievably friendly."

"I really enjoyed the smaller towns in New Brunswick, in those areas the people were great and supportive."

QUEBEC

June 10 to 27
18 Days
398 Miles

Marathon Total:

1,850 Miles

Marathon of Hope
Quebec
Actual Route

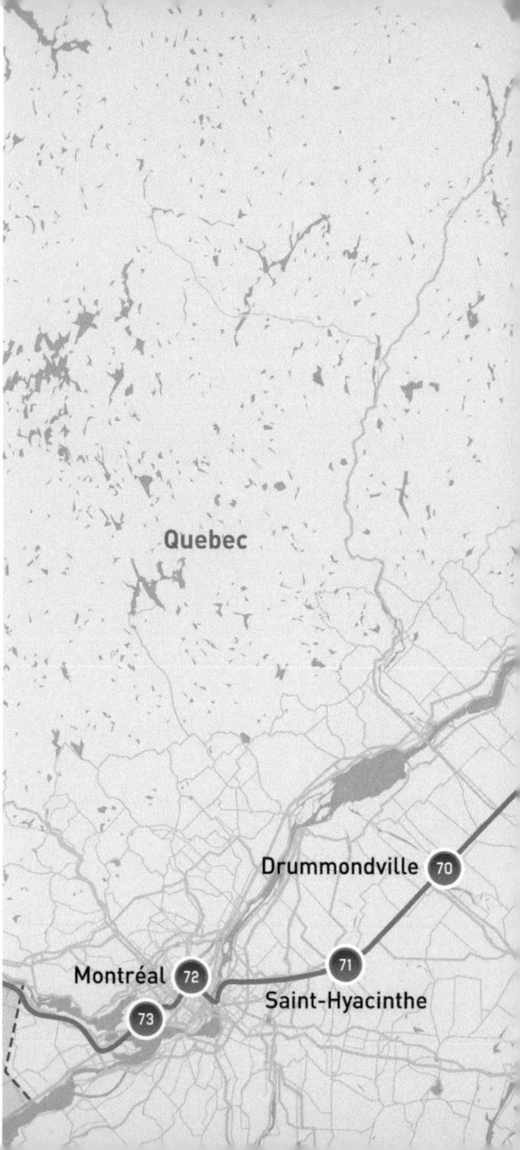

Quebec

Drummondville 70

Montréal 72

71

Saint-Hyacinthe

73

St. Lawrence River

62 Rivière-du-Loup

New Brunswick

Québec City

66

United States

69

"We went to the Holiday Inn in Sainte-Foy. We were warmly greeted by press and society. It seemed as if they are going to get something done for the rest of the way in Quebec."

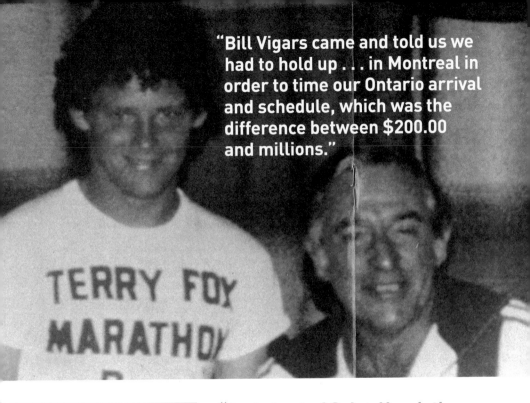

"Bill Vigars came and told us we had to hold up . . . in Montreal in order to time our Ontario arrival and schedule, which was the difference between $200.00 and millions."

June 21, 1980
Day 71
Saint-Hyacinthe, Quebec

"Just short of Saint-Hyacinthe I had a beautiful shower and meal. We met Gérard Côté, the 4 time Boston Marathon winner. What an honour!"

"Here with other runners and eventually Don Sweet and some wheelchair guys I ran to the Four Seasons Hotel on Sherbrooke Street. There was a warm reception here, and lots of media."

June 22, 1980
Day 72
Montréal, Quebec

"Today I took off because I have spare time getting into Ontario."

"It's not like they're not friendly here. It's just they don't know what I'm doing. People drive by and stop to ask if I want a ride."

"You know anyone can get cancer. I'm running across Canada and Quebec is a province of Canada . . . With me it isn't political or racial. I'm just a human being and cancer can strike anyone and I'm trying to help everyone on my run."

ONTARIO

June 28 to September 1
66 Days
1,489 Miles

Marathon Total:
3,339 Miles

Marathon of Hope
Ontario
Actual Route

Ontario

Quebec

Sudbury 115

Hawkesbury 78

Ottawa 81

Gravenhurst 108

Lake Huron

Toronto 91

Lake Ontario

London 97

United States

Lake Erie

"I rested before running over the bridge into Hawkesbury at 12:30 p.m. Here we had a very warm welcome waiting. Lots of people greeted me and I did my speech."

June 28, 1980
Day 78
Hawkesbury, Ontario

"I ran with police and others to the Governor General's house and met Mr. Schreyer and his wife. After this I ran to Sparks Street Mall where I had a tremendous unbelievable welcome! Very heartwarming! I really flew. I did 5 more miles, all with police escort and incredible support from the people. The best welcome so far."

81

"I went to the Ottawa–Saskatoon football game where I kicked off the opening ball, to a standing ovation."

"After that standing ovation at the CFL game, I could hardly believe it. It makes me feel like people really care about what I'm doing and that it's all worthwhile."

July 1, 1980
Day 81
Ottawa, Ontario

"I met Mr. Trudeau. It was an honour and he is a very nice man. Unfortunately he is very busy and couldn't run with me."

84

"Ran all the way through Oshawa. Had a marvelous reception. Sensational. People lined the streets all the way. Then I had a great reception at the local mall with a marching band. Simply nothing like it before."

"You are a tremendous inspiration to me. You don't know what you've done for me. Thank You."

"I met my parents and Judy in a surprise reunion at 3 miles."

"I didn't expect to see them until London!"

"My family is here, whether they're with me or not . . . When you're running all day long you don't really get to visit. You're in a different mental frame and if you're thinking about relaxing and enjoying, it makes running more difficult."

July 10, 1980
Day 90
Whitby, Ontario

"I went to a very emotional reception at Scarborough where I did my best speech."

87

"A cute girl with cancer gave me a rose and it broke me up."

"I've said to people before that I'm going to do my very best to make it, I'm not going to give up, and that's true. But I might not make it. And if I don't make it, the Marathon of Hope better continue."

"I ran to Nathan Phillips Square. Thousands of people cheered me on. Estimated 10,000!"

July 11, 1980
Day 91
Toronto, Ontario

"This is unreal,
beautiful —
the best ever."

"We went to
my room where
I met Fred,
which was a
shocker, and then
Darryl Sittler,
a great man."

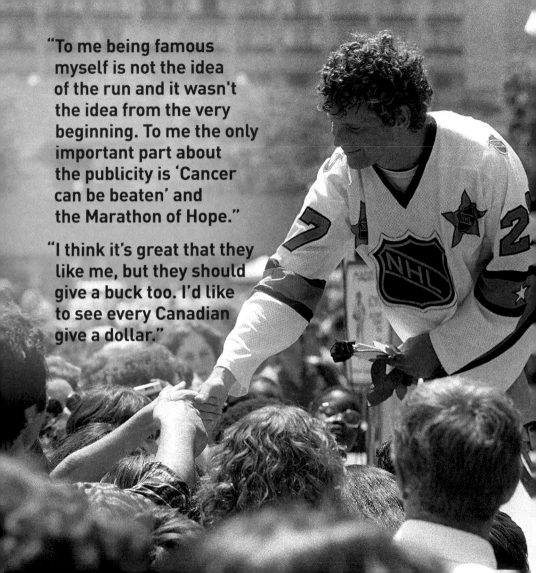

"To me being famous myself is not the idea of the run and it wasn't the idea from the very beginning. To me the only important part about the publicity is 'Cancer can be beaten' and the Marathon of Hope."

"I think it's great that they like me, but they should give a buck too. I'd like to see every Canadian give a dollar."

"A lady brought a little guy up to meet me. She explained that he had cancer. She told me to keep going — that I was doing something great for her son."

"Greg Scott's an inspiration to me too. I'll never forget that meeting."

July 14, 1980
Day 94
Hamilton, Ontario

"I made it to Woodstock where the whole town was out to greet me. Then with Ron Calhoun we drove to Thamesford for a reception, back to Woodstock for a dinner reception and then back to Thamesford to Ron's to sleep."

"We drove to London where I ran through the city 4 miles to the park reception. It was great, people were out all the way, the roads were packed, and there were thousands in the park. Tony Coutinho ran the final mile with me."

July 17, 1980
Day 97
London, Ontario

"Today was hard because I had so many interruptions."

"We went back to St. Marys for a beautiful reception. The whole town was out."

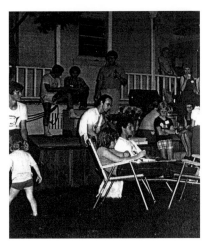

"Today was short because of a great reception with corporate executives in Toronto. I left a good impression and did one of my best speeches. Later we met and ate dinner with Bobby Orr, the highlight of my trip. He is a very nice man."

"Bobby, you were the greatest hockey player in the world and if it would help you play again, I'd gladly offer you my good knee and I'd still find a way to get to Vancouver."

July 23, 1980
Day 103
Toronto, Ontario

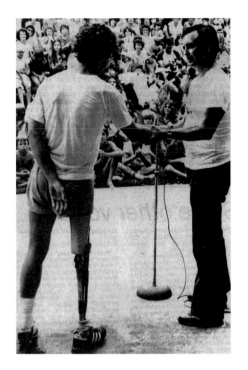

"Today was a great day!
Went to the Holiday Inn
for a birthday party
and cake fight."

"You people have really given me something else.
I've had a lot of receptions, but I can't believe this.
I'll never forget this birthday."

"I went to Beaver Creek
prison for a reception
and then a wonderful
birthday party in
Gravenhurst. The Civic
Centre was full and there
was a band and everybody
sang happy birthday.
Thorough enjoyment."

July 28, 1980
Day 108
Gravenhurst, Ontario

"I was bothered all day by people from the media worried about my stump because Cliff Chadderton said I was hurting myself. Everybody is so worried, even Leslie came up to make sure I was O.K."

"If you read in the papers that Terry Fox is tired, he's down and he's out, don't dare believe it. I'm not going to quit."

"I've seen people in so much pain, so sore. The little bit of pain I'm going through is nothing. They can't shut it off and I can't shut down every time I feel a little sore."

July 30, 1980
Day 110
Bala, Ontario

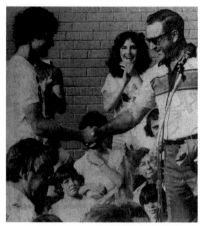

"It was great running through here. We met Bobby Orr's dad and he gave me Bobby's Canada Cup sweater which is something unbelievable. Greatest gift I've ever been given."

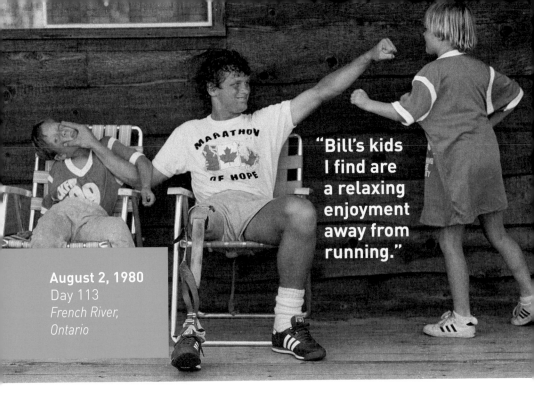

"Bill's kids I find are a relaxing enjoyment away from running."

August 2, 1980
Day 113
French River,
Ontario

"There can be no reason for me to stop. No matter what pain I suffer, it is nothing compared to the pain of those who have cancer, and of those who endure treatment, often with little or no hope of recovery."

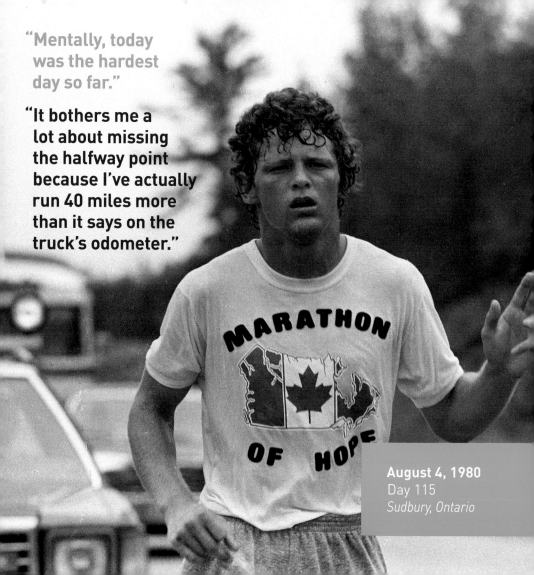

"Mentally, today was the hardest day so far."

"It bothers me a lot about missing the halfway point because I've actually run 40 miles more than it says on the truck's odometer."

August 4, 1980
Day 115
Sudbury, Ontario

"I have a swollen and painful ankle. Worried."

August 20

"My ankle killed me in the afternoon. More swollen. I am starting to worry. Somehow I think it will go away on its own!"

August 21

"Today my ankle got worse. By 17 miles I couldn't take it anymore. I am worried, upset, desperate. It could all be finished!"

August 22

"Found out I have tendonitis and should be able to keep going on Monday."

August 23

"Today we slept in and I again rested my ankle."

August 24

"Today my ankle was tender and sore but not near as bad. So thankful to be able to keep going! Thanks goodness no stress fracture!"

August 25

Days 131 to 136
Near Marathon, Ontario

August 23, 1980
Terry with OPP officer Reg Essa at the Marathon Ontario airport. Terry flew back to Sault Ste. Marie for an ankle X-ray.

"Today was a good day. Greg and his parents came. I ran in a lake with Greg and the others after. Was fun."

"This is why I do it. Little kids like him shouldn't have to go through this stuff."

"Greg rode his bike behind me for about 6 miles and it has to be the most inspirational moment I have had! The first 13 were hard but I made it! At night we had a beautiful reception in Terrace Bay. I spoke about Greg and couldn't hold back the emotion."

"I wish he could be here with me all the time, for the rest of the trip."

August 27, 1980
Day 138
Terrace Bay, Ontario

"In Ontario the response and friendliness of all the people has been almost overwhelming."

September 1, 1980
Day 143
Outside Thunder Bay, Ontario

"I had run, I think it was 13 miles, in the morning, felt good, felt real good, I had a good morning run. It was not raining but it was a cloudy day."

"Then I slept a couple of hours, came back out, went to where I'd left off."

"By now there were all kinds of people, tons of people lining the road waiting for me."

"At this point I guess I was about 18 miles and I went out, started running, still felt pretty good. I think it was starting to drizzle rain a bit. People were cheering me on all the way for the whole 8 miles that I did in the afternoon."

"When I finished my 5th mile I started coughing and I went into the van and I was lying down taking a drink, taking a bit of a break. I started coughing and all of a sudden coughing really, really hard and then felt a pain in my neck that spread down into my chest."

"I didn't know what to do but I went out and ran because it was the only thing to do."

"And I was running with this pain in my chest and I began to think. You know, there's something wrong. This may be my last mile . . . And I ran that mile and I got in the van and I said to Doug, 'will you drive me to the hospital. I've got to go and it's not my ankle, it's not my foot.'"

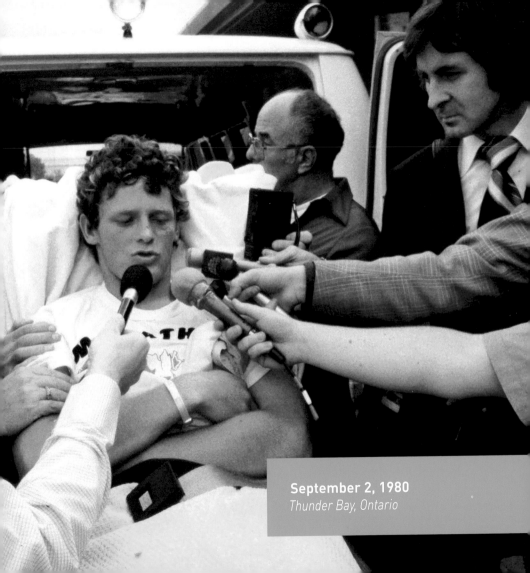

September 2, 1980
Thunder Bay, Ontario

AFTER THE RUN

"Originally I had primary cancer in my knee, 3½ years ago and . . . the cancer had spread. And now I've got cancer in my lungs. And we gotta go home, and try and do some more treatment. But, all I can say is that if there's any way I can get out there again and finish it I will."

City says goodbye to Terry

Nation mourns Terry

June 28, 1981

"Even though I die of cancer, my spirit didn't die and I kept trying, and that should influence a lot of people as well."

ACKNOWLEDGEMENTS

This publication is issued in conjunction with the exhibition
Terry Fox - Running to the Heart of Canada at the Canadian Museum of History (April 1, 2015 – January 24, 2016), organized in collaboration with the Terry Fox Centre for the 35th anniversary of the Marathon of Hope.

Exhibition Team

Curator:
Sheldon Posen

Creative Developer:
Claire Champ

Research Associate:
Erin Gurski

Scenographers:
Marie-Claude Baillargeon, Chantal Baril

Audio-Visual Specialist:
Dave Deevey

Graphic Designers:
Visou Design, Stéphane Breton

Project Managers:
Jean-Luc Desjardins, Yves Poirier

Research Assistants:
Nathalie Wright, Nellie James, Ivan Jozepovic

Special Thanks

Darrell Fox, Judith Fox, Fred Fox;
Doug Alward; Bill Vigars; Ron Calhoun;
Leslie Scrivener; Gail Harvey; Isadore Sharp;
Marnie Burnham, Gillian Pedwell, Caitlin Webster,
Library and Archives Canada, Burnaby, B.C.;
Allison Mailer, BC Sports Hall of Fame;
The Terry Fox Centre; The Terry Fox Foundation;
The Terry Fox Research Institute.

THE EXHIBITION

Terry Fox - Running to the Heart of Canada is an extensive display of memorabilia and audio-visual materials relating to one of the most beloved and culturally important figures in modern Canadian history. The exhibition invites visitors to relive the Marathon of Hope and to experience the extraordinary effect Terry Fox had on Canada and Canadians during his 143-day run to raise money for cancer research. It explores Terry Fox's legacy in the decades since.

Artifacts on display include Terry Fox's hand-written journal, artificial leg, Marathon T-shirts, running shoes and other gear. Visitors can browse or search scans of the thousands of cards and letters sent to Terry. And they can see and hear how Terry Fox's story has become part of Canada's physical landscape, part of its popular culture, and part of the way Canadians define who they are.

Photo Credits

Scrapbooks

Courtesy of the family of Terry Fox. Scrapbooks by Mimi Curtis (Oshawa, Ont.), Betty Booth (Delta, B.C.), Mrs. Judy Fountain (Gravenhurst, Ont.), Mary Ann Wark (Melita, Man.), Dave Steward (Toronto, Ont.), Gladys Nolan (London, Ont.) and Terry's mother, Betty Fox (Port Coquitlam, B.C.).

© Gail Harvey: Inside front cover;
p. 4; p. 6; p. 14; p. 16; p. 101; p. 102; p. 115

© Boris Spremo: p. 3; p. 38; p. 76; p. 99;
p. 105 [right]; p. 107

© Canadian Museum of History:
p. 7 (Marie-Louise Deruaz); p. 18 (Steven Darby)

© *The Province* (Vancouver, B.C.):
p. 8 (Colin Price); p. 114

© *The Vancouver Sun*: p. 10 (Ralph Bower); p. 114

© Torstar Syndication Services
(Reprinted with permission): p. 17

© *Ottawa Citizen*: p. 22 (Chris Mikula);
p. 81 [bottom left]; p. 108; p. 112; p. 114

© *Toronto Star*: p. 26; p. 29; p. 70; p. 84 [left];
p. 86 [top] (Erin Combs); p. 87 [top left]
(Michael Stuparyk); p. 96 [bottom] (David Cooper);
p. 110-111 (The Canadian Press/David Cooper); p. 112

© CP Images: p. 27-28 (Dick Green); p. 40; p. 44 [right]; p. 66 (Jacques Nadeau); p. 82 [bottom] (Drew Gregg); p. 83 [right] (Rod MacIvor); p. 83 [left] (Peter Bregg); p. 89 (Bill Becker); p. 90 [bottom left, bottom right] (Bill Becker); p. 91 (Bill Becker); p. 96 [top] (Globe and Mail/Staff Photographer); p. 105 [left] (Boris Spremo)

© Photo Features: p. 30; p. 80

© The Four Seasons Hotels and Resorts: p. 31

© *The Grand Falls Advertiser*: p. 32-34

© *The Western Star* (Corner Brook, N.L.): p. 35-36

© *The Gulf News* (Port Aux Basques, N.L.): p. 37

© *The Georgian* (Bay St. George, N.L.): p. 39

© *Cape Breton Post*: p. 44 [left]

© *The Victoria Times*: p. 45

© *The Chronicle-Herald* (Halifax, N.S.): p. 48-49

© *Truro Daily News*: p. 50

© *Amherst Daily News*: p. 51

© *The Guardian* (Charlottetown, P.E.I.):
p. 52; p. 57 [right]

© *The Evening-Patriot* (Charlottetown, P.E.I.): p. 56

© *The Telegraph-Journal* (Saint John, N.B.): p. 58